COPYRIGHTS

GETTING RIGHT WITH MONEY

Principles about money from King Solomon, the wisest, richest man ever, to help you have more money, need less money, and have your life be bigger than money

THANK YOU

Thanks to the many people who have graced me with experience and insight on money matters throughout the years. Special thanks to William Radigan, Robert and Elizabeth Esping, Ron Williams, Gideon Grafe, David Brittain, and Lynda Grafe for reviewing this and helping refine it; I only hope that the final version includes enough of your many good ideas. Thanks are also due to everyone who reads this and puts any of Solomon's principles into action; getting right with money makes your life better, and makes the life of everyone around you better, too.

TABLE OF CONTENTS

GO BEYOND THE COOKBOOK

There are two levels of understanding for most activities. At the first level, you know just enough to be able to follow someone else's instructions. You know what tablespoons and cups are, and you have the basic ingredients on hand, so you can follow a recipe and cook something that hopefully looks like the picture in the book.

When you can cook by following recipes, you have access to a wide range of foods; there are more cookbooks and recipes than you could ever try. However, no recipe can ever fully anticipate your objectives for the meal (feeding 1 or 100? Impressing the boss or stuffing the soccer team?), or the ingredients you have on hand (can you substitute thyme for salt? What do you do if you're out of baking powder?), or your particular skills and tools (good at stirring but bad at whipping? What if you don't have a 9x9 baking pan?).

In the world of personal money management, there are a lot of recipes out there: step by step plans for making more money, 5 easy steps to pay off debt, 7 weird tricks to save money at the grocery store. Following a recipe is certainly better than having no plan at all, but it is not where you really need to be. No money recipe can anticipate your unique financial situation. No money recipe can fully account for your unique life setting, or take full advantage of the strengths and opportunities you have, or adjust for your individual weaknesses. Worse, even if you found such a recipe, you would be living a financial life dictated by the author of the recipe. You want to live your own life, and being able to manage your own money is part of that.

True mastery of your personal finances requires that you go beyond following recipes. You need to become a chef. Chefs are able to make their own food plans on the fly; they are able to mix and match ingredients and dishes to create the meal they want. They understand the principles of food well enough that they can adapt when a spice jar is unexpectedly empty, or extra guests show up, or someone reveals a food allergy at the last minute, or the oven won't heat over 400 degrees tonight.

You want to be a chef in dealing with money. You want to understand the principles of money well enough that you can create the outcomes you want. You want to be able to think correctly about money, so that you can consider your own situation, make your own plans, and carry them out. You want to have the right relationship with your money so that you use it as a tool, instead of following someone else's directions. While there is no single magic recipe for financial success for everyone, there are some principles that are the starting point for any sound financial plan.

As you read on, you will discover six principles that King Solomon, the wisest and richest man ever, taught us about money. I will use examples with rounded numbers to illustrate the principles, and I doubt that any of the examples exactly match your situation. That's fine, even good, since you don't need another detailed recipe that doesn't match your life. You need to be able to figure out how to apply the principles to your life. Understanding the principles, and figuring out how to apply them every day in your life, will put you in control of your finances.

King Solomon also told us something more important about our relationship with money. Living according to Solomon's first six principles will make you a much better money manager, but your life should be much more than money. Solomon's last principle teaches us the right relationship to money; getting that relationship right is essential to living a life that is much more than money.

I have found that, when faced with a difficult problem, it is most important to keep in mind the right principles that need to guide your thinking, Decisions that are in line with the right principles are likely to succeed; those that violate the right principles are likely to fail. Solomon's teachings are those right principles about money. I hope that this book enables you to have the right attitudes about money, so that you can keep those in mind as you make decisions about money matters. These principles will let you be the master of your money, instead of its slave.

ADVICE FROM THE WISEST, RICHEST MAN EVER

You don't become a chef by memorizing recipes. You become a chef by understanding the principles behind cooking. You become a chef by learning how to think about food like a great chef thinks about food. You become expert at managing your money by learning to think about money like a wise person thinks about money.

I want to share with you some advice about money from the wisest, richest man ever. I may have some wisdom, and some riches, but I make no claim to being the wisest, richest man ever. But King Solomon was. So this book is not my advice, but just my retelling of Solomon's principles about money, translated and applied to today's world.

King Solomon had a lot of money, a whole lot of money. He also had wisdom; according to the book of Kings, Solomon had the most wise and discerning heart there ever was or ever will be (1 Kings 3:12). So Solomon's advice about money is from the wisest man there ever was, and from a man who had practical experience with lots of money.

King Solomon was a king of Israel, and inherited and generated wealth beyond what most of us can imagine. Let's look at his finances, as reported in the Biblical books of Chronicles and Kings and using today's valuations:

Annual income - $1 billion in gold, plus more from traders, merchants, neighboring countries (2 Chronicles 9).

Inheritance - $11 billion plus. (1 Chronicles 29).

From his dad to build the Temple: Over $4 billion in gold and silver, plus all the bronze, iron, wood, onyx and antimony he needed, plus precious stones and alabaster in abundance (1 Chronicles 29:1-5).

Given by others to build the Temple: Over $7 billion in gold and silver, plus 675 tons of brass and 4,000 tons of iron, plus uncounted precious stones (1 Chronicles 29:6-9).

Gift from the Queen of Sheba - about $200 million in gold, plus spices. (2 Chronicles 9)

Income from expedition to Ophira – almost $600 million in gold. (1 Kings 9)

He also received gold and silver, ivory and apes and peacocks from Hiram every three years. Every one of his cups was made of gold; none was of silver (1 Kings 10). He made silver and gold as plentiful in Jerusalem as stones, and he made cedars as plentiful as sycamores in the lowland (1 Chronicles 1).

His house took 13 years to build. He employed over 150,000 men to build the Temple and his house (2 Chronicles 2). That's more than the total employment of Disney. Think Disneyland, Disney World, Epcot, Wild Animal Kingdom, Disney cruises, ... - all for building his house.

Solomon knew about money, and as a king he also knew about people. Though he lived a long time ago, he was not an uneducated rustic, squatting by a fire and eating sheep on a stick. He was one of the wealthiest men ever to live.

But as rich as Solomon was, money was not his goal. God offered Solomon anything he wanted (1 Kings 3). Solomon replied by admitting that he was like a child, not up to the task of being king. Solomon asked for an understanding heart, to be able to discern good and evil. God was so pleased with Solomon's request that God gave Solomon a wise and discerning heart, the most wise and discerning heart there ever was or ever will be. God also added riches and honor, so that Solomon would stand out among all kings.

There are a lot of rich people who are not wise. And, there are a lot of people who are wise about some things but don't have experience with money. King Solomon had riches above almost everyone who has ever lived, and had wisdom above everyone who has ever lived. And, good for us, he wrote down his best advice about money in the Biblical book of Proverbs.

The book of Proverbs is the most complete, concise collection of practical and spiritual advice about daily life. I can personally verify that it is right on target when it comes to money matters. I have advised, helped found, invested in, represented, managed, and done deals with hundreds of businesses. I've had business meetings with extremely wealthy individuals, famous money managers and noted investors. I've read stacks of finance and business books. None of those matches the book of Proverbs for true and practical advice. Every bit of good advice from all those others is already in

Proverbs. The rest of this writing will focus on some simple principles from Proverbs that are easy to understand, and that will absolutely change your financial life if you understand them and put them into practice.

Solomon's advice will help you get money, but it's not about getting rich quickly. It's not even primarily about getting rich. His advice is about the right relationship between you and money. In the book of Proverbs, Solomon gives us six important principles about how we manage our money, and a seventh principle that is critical for living in a wise relationship with money. I encourage you to take his advice to heart, to make it part of you. So many problems become easy once you look at them the right way – Solomon's advice will help you look at money problems the right way. Too much debt, too little income, worry about whether you have enough money – Solomon's advice will give you the wisdom to handle those problems and more.

Before we can understand Solomon's principles about money, we have to get the right attitude about money itself.

MONEY IS NOT THE GOAL (BUT IT CAN HELP)

A question for you: Do you want to have more money? Many people will say yes. Others will think yes but say no because it feels more holy to say no. I don't think it's wrong to say yes, but there's a lot more to understand first.

Before you can decide whether you want to have more money, you have to know what money really is. A full explanation takes a lot more than we need to understand Solomon's advice, but we do need at least an overview. Let's start with a more basic question: what is your life about? What do you accomplish each day? Anything you do that is opposite God's desires is ultimately worthless, so your real objective every day is to accomplish what God wants to happen. This includes things like providing for your family, helping others, and enjoying beauty. This applies to you even if you don't believe in God – if you believe that your life matters, then there must be some organizing principle of the universe, and your actions are ultimately weighed in conformance to that principle. If you don't believe in God, and you don't believe that your life matters, then there is no point to anything you do, including reading this book. I am sad for you, and I hope that soon you will find a better reason to live. When you do, then come back to this book to learn how to live better.

Now how do you go about accomplishing God's purposes? The simple path is you work directly on something that fits God's plan. The slightly more complicated path involves money – you work for someone else, they give you money, then you use that money to pay for something that accomplishes God's purposes. Money is just an *intermediate form*, a way to translate one thing you do into another thing done by someone else. You start at your starting place (time and resources), then trade those for money, then trade the money to get to your goal place. Money is not relevant to your true starting place and goal place; money is just a usually convenient way to get from start to goal.

Once you realize that, then "For the love of money is a root of all sorts of evil, and some by longing for it have wandered away from the faith and pierced themselves with many griefs" (1 Timothy 6:10 NASB) becomes more clear. If you love the intermediate form, then you lose sight of the real objective. The Bible makes this clear in several other writings. "He who loves money will not be satisfied with money" (Ecclesiastes 5:10 NASB).

However, if you understand money as just an intermediate form, then money can be good. "It is the blessing of the Lord that makes rich, And He adds no sorrow to it" (Proverbs 10:22 NASB). "… as for every man to whom God has given riches and wealth, He has also empowered him to eat from them and to receive his reward and rejoice in his labor; this is the gift of God"

(Ecclesiastes 5:19 NASB). If God gives riches and wealth, it is so that you can eat from them. Money is a blessing only as an intermediate form on the way to doing something else that is good.

OK, money is an intermediate form. But you still want and need it. How do you get more of this "intermediate form?" And what do you do with it once you have it? Solomon gives us six principles about money that we must understand: three things you shouldn't do, and three things you should do instead. We'll introduce the three "should nots," then the three "shoulds," then go back over them in more detail with examples of how to apply to your life. Last, and most important, we'll cover the final bit of wisdom from Solomon that is essential to keeping money in its proper place.

THREE THINGS YOU SHOULD NOT DO

Solomon's advice is really pretty simple stuff. You could call it common sense. It does make sense, but unfortunately it's not all that common. Most people don't listen to the best advice about money, and then they are distressed about being poor. It's a little sad, because the desire to get money is common, but the willingness to do what God says about it is rare. Solomon gives us three "don'ts" in relation to money:

1. Don't go into debt.
2. Don't try to get rich quickly, or by cheating.
3. Don't be lazy.

1. DON'T GO INTO DEBT

Solomon's first advice is to stay out of debt. The advice comes in two parts. First, if you borrow and do not pay back, then you're wicked. So, if you borrow, you have to pay it back.

"The wicked borrows and does not pay back." (Psalm 37:21 NASB).

Second, until you pay back what you've borrowed, you are the lender's slave.

"The borrower becomes the lender's slave." (Proverbs 22:7 NASB).

Is this true? Does the borrower really become the lender's slave? Think about how money works – you work for someone, and they give you money in return. But when you borrow, you take the money before you do the work. Now you must do the work, regardless of whether you want to do the work. If you have to work for someone, against your present wishes, then you are a slave. Once you borrow money, you have enslaved yourself. Paying off any debt, or even better paying off all your debt, is a wonderful feeling. It's hard to describe the feeling of being freed from debt slavery; I hope you get to experience it.

Is this applicable to today's world, though? How can you live in the modern world and not borrow money? Is it possible to buy a house, a car, or a major appliance without debt? How do you pay for a nice vacation without putting it on your credit card? Read Solomon's warning again. It's not a prohibition against debt. It is just a warning that debt enslaves you. So if you are willing to be enslaved, for a time, to buy the house you want, then go ahead. But think hard about whether the vacation is worth being enslaved. And in any case do all you can to pay it off, to get out of slavery as soon as you can.

Consider some numbers. If you have a $50,000 annual income, and spend $50,000 a year, you have no debt, no slavery. If you spend $55,000 on a $50,000 income, you have to borrow

$5,000 to make up for your overspending. If you overspend by $5,000 each year, and pay just 10% interest, in year ten you are almost $70,000 in debt, and have to borrow $12,000 just to pay for that year's overspending plus interest on the previous years' borrowing. If the lender stops lending, you have to cut your lifestyle by 25% just to cover the interest on your existing debt.

According to the U.S. Census Bureau, median U.S. household debt in 2011 was about $70,000. That's a lot of slavery. Don't be a slave.

2. DON'T TRY TO GET RICH QUICKLY, OR GET RICH BY CHEATING

Solomon give us several warnings that trying to get money by cheating is a bad idea. The money won't stay with you, and the cheating will destroy you.

"Wealth obtained by fraud will dwindle, but whoever earns it through labor will multiply it." (Proverbs 13:11 HCSB).

"Making a fortune through a lying tongue is a vanishing mist, a pursuit of death." (Proverbs 21:6 HCSB).

"The righteousness of the upright will deliver them, But the treacherous will be caught by their own greed." (Proverbs 11:6 NASB).

"Bread obtained by falsehood is sweet to a man, But afterward his mouth will be filled with gravel." (Proverbs 20:17 NASB).

"But he who makes haste to be rich will not go unpunished." (Proverbs 28:20 NASB).

It's common to think that winning the lottery would make your money problems go away. Solomon warns us that getting rich quickly doesn't work. And experience shows it doesn't work. Big winners of lotteries win, on average, more than enough to pay off all their current debt. But lottery winners are about twice as likely to file for bankruptcy as others. It seems backwards, but getting rich quickly leads lottery winners to bankruptcy.

It's also tempting to cheat to get money. This doesn't work, either. If people see through your scam, you lose your reputation (and chance to honestly earn money from them) and don't get any money. You might cheat some people, only to get caught by the law, and end up losing your physical freedom as well as whatever money you might have gained. You might get money, and evade legal consequences, but you are even worse off than the lottery winner – you have money without wisdom to manage it, and you have sacrificed your character. You are a terrible person who happens to have money, and no amount of money can buy back your self-respect.

But what about people who get money by cheating, or by get rich quick schemes, and don't get punished? This is a critical point to recognize – **it doesn't happen**. Just because you don't see the punishment or consequence, doesn't mean there is no punishment or consequence. God doesn't say that fraud **should** be punished, or that wealth obtained by fraud will **probably** dwindle. He says it **will** happen, and so it will, whether we observe it or not. Consequences that are not visible to us still exist.

Trying to lie, cheat, or steal your way to money does not work. Remember that money is an intermediate form on the way to doing God's will. You can't walk with God when you start off in the opposite direction.

3. DON'T BE LAZY

Solomon's third "don't" is a warning against being lazy. He tells us the simple truth that, if you are lazy, you won't have enough.

"A little sleep, a little slumber, a little folding of the arms to rest, and your poverty will come like a robber, your need, like a bandit." (Proverbs 24:33 HCSB).

"The sluggard does not plow after the autumn, So he begs during the harvest and has nothing." (Proverbs 20:4 NASB).

"Do not love sleep, or you will become poor; Open your eyes, and you will be satisfied with food." (Proverbs 20:13 NASB).

You can probably come up with your own examples for this one. The basic idea is no work, no money. A lot of scams are built on the appeal of getting money for nothing. If someone offers you money by encouraging you to be lazy, then they are asking you to believe that God lies. Laziness doesn't work.

THREE THINGS YOU SHOULD DO

Avoiding the three negatives helps you avoid a lot of money troubles. Solomon also gives us three things to do that lead us to the right relationship with money:

1. Plan ahead.
2. Work.
3. Spend wisely.

1. PLAN AHEAD

Managing Solomon's kingdom, and managing Solomon's immense wealth, required Solomon's wisdom to plan ahead. His shipments of gold and silver, ivory and apes and peacocks from Hiram came every three years, so he had to plan for uneven income. Solomon tells us that planning ahead is important for success:

"Carefully consider the path for your feet, and all your ways will be established," (Proverbs 4:26 HCSB).

He tells us several other times to plan ahead, first by pointing out that ants do it, then warning that working without a plan brings poverty.

"Go to the ant, O sluggard, Observe her ways and be wise, Which, having no chief, Officer or ruler, Prepares her food in the summer And gathers her provision in the harvest." (Proverbs 6:6-8 NASB).

"The plans of the diligent lead surely to advantage, But everyone who is hasty comes surely to poverty." (Proverbs 21:5 NASB).

Solomon even gives us a basic financial plan - tend to our fields (the way we make our living) before we build our house (the place we rest):

"Prepare your work outside And make it ready for yourself in the field; Afterwards, then, build your house." (Proverbs 24:27 NASB).

Animals live moment to moment. We experience life in time, but God has given us the ability to see beyond the present time.

"He has also set eternity in their heart." (Ecclesiastes 3:11 NASB).

Plan ahead, envision the future and work toward it. That is part of being made in God's image. Failure to plan is often the first step of failure in money matters (and in most of life).

2. WORK

Solomon already told us not to be lazy. His instruction to work is the counterpart to his warning against laziness. "Don't be lazy" is just a warning, though, while the advice to work comes with a promise: if you work, then you will have enough.

"The Lord will not allow the righteous to hunger, But He will reject the craving of the wicked. Poor is he who works with a negligent hand, But the hand of the diligent makes rich. He who gathers in summer is a son who acts wisely, But he who sleeps in harvest is a son who acts shamefully." (Proverbs 10:3-5 NASB).

"He who tills his land will have plenty of bread, But he who pursues worthless things lacks sense." (Proverbs 12:11 NASB).

"The hand of the diligent will rule, But the slack hand will be put to forced labor." (Proverbs 12:24 NASB).

"In all labor there is profit, But mere talk leads only to poverty." (Proverbs 14:23 NASB).

Read Proverbs 12:11 again and imagine a young person working at an entry level job, getting started on a lifetime of knowing how to work. And then imagine another young person, unwilling to work, hanging out with friends, playing video games in the parents' basement. You know, even without reading Proverbs, that the first person will have plenty of bread, and know that the second person will not.

We know that crime and injustice can make people poor, even people who work. Resisting crime and oppression is important, but Solomon's promise of "if you work, you have enough" still stands. Whatever your surroundings, you will have more if you work than if you are lazy.

3. SPEND WISELY

Part of dealing with money is spending it. In fact, if you don't eventually spend it, then money is worthless. Solomon tells us that spending too much on pleasure will make you poor.

"He who loves pleasure will become a poor man; He who loves wine and oil will not become rich." (Proverbs 21:17 NASB).

"For the heavy drinker and the glutton will come to poverty, And drowsiness will clothe one with rags." (Proverbs 23:21 NASB).

You can probably come up with your own examples of why this is important. Living in New Mexico, I'm amused when I see a boat for sale. 100 miles from the nearest place that might float it, who would buy it? But the current owner did. For a more personal exercise, think about the stuff in your house that clutters up a closet, or the garage. Think about all the stuff you would like to put in a garage sale, or donate. Now think back to when buying that item was so important to you. And count up the money you could have saved, and closet or garage space you'd still have open if you hadn't bought it.

PUTTING SOLOMON'S PRINCIPLES INTO PRACTICE IN YOUR LIFE

We will take the next few chapters to work through applications of Solomon's advice to life today. Everyone's situation is different, but you should see some ways to use Solomon's advice to make your life better. First, let's get out of the bad habits that let money be our master instead of our servant.

DON'T GO INTO DEBT

Solomon warns us that the borrower becomes the lender's slave. In today's financial system, there are some kinds of debt that might not be enslaving. To apply the "avoid debt" principle to our financial lives today, we have to dig a little deeper into what debt is, and better understand how it enslaves.

DOES ALL DEBT ENSLAVE?

Most personal debt is "recourse debt." A lender can collect from any asset of the borrower to recover a recourse debt. If the lender is limited to a specific asset, then the debt is nonrecourse. Recourse debts always trigger Solomon's warning about slavery. A non-recourse debt might not. This distinction is sometimes used to try to pretend that debt is not enslaving, so we need to see through this mirage first.

A non-recourse debt is typically used to purchase a specific valuable asset, such as a car or house. If the loan is not repaid, then the lender can take the asset instead. If the asset is valuable enough, then the lender takes back the asset and cancels the loan, so the debt did not enslave you. If the asset is not valuable enough to cover the debt (sometimes called being "upside down" on a loan), then we hit the question of whether the debt is of the enslaving kind. If the lender can recover the deficiency from other assets, then the loan is really a recourse debt and it is enslaving. If the lender is stuck with whatever the asset is worth, then the debt is non-recourse, and might not be enslaving. We are not out of the enslavement woods yet, though.

Even if the lender is limited to the specific asset, a non-recourse debt can still be enslaving if you are not willing to part with the asset. For example, if you have a home mortgage, and it is truly non-recourse, then all you lose if you don't pay the debt is the house. However, if you are not willing to walk away from the house (where will your family live?), then the debt is still enslaving. As a contrary example, if you have a non-recourse debt on a tractor used on your farm, and you can continue life without the tractor, then that debt is not enslaving.

This is a finer distinction than is needed in real life. Few lenders will loan to individuals with only the security of a single asset; they almost always get a claim against all of your assets to guarantee the loan. Consequently, almost all personal and consumer debt is recourse debt. Also, most people don't want to part with things like cars and houses, so we'll consider all debt as enslaving debt from here on. Be very careful if you think you have a debt that is exempt from Solomon's warning about enslavement.

DEBT IS NOT PROHIBITED

Despite how I worded the first of Solomon's principles, I have to admit that Proverbs doesn't really say "Don't go into debt." Solomon just warns us that "the borrower becomes the lender's slave." So the real warning from Solomon is to avoid being enslaved.

In today's world, it can be quite difficult to buy a house without borrowing money. In some parts of the U.S., cars are essential to daily life, and it can be hard to buy your first car with money you haven't yet earned. Many people borrow money for school, thinking that the education will enable them to earn the money to repay the student loans.

These can all be reasonable financial decisions. Solomon's warning, though, gives you the right framework for decision. If you are going to borrow money to go to school, you must realize that you are enslaved to earn the money to repay the loan. Your decision to borrow $10,000 for school is also a commitment to earn $10,000 (plus interest) when you graduate, and pay that to the lender. It's not a $10,000 **borrowing decision**; it's a $10,000 **work commitment**. If you borrow money for a car or house, you are making similar work commitments.

If you make that decision, or if you've already made it, don't sugarcoat the fact that you are enslaved. Do all you can to get released from the slavery. I say this not only from Proverbs but also from personal experience. We built the home where we raised our family. We built the cabinets. Our family worked together to build fences and lay walkways. Parts of the yard are referred to as "the old pig pen" or "where we buried the dog." There are a lot of shared memories in that home. But we were at risk of losing all that as long as we owed money on it. We never wanted to lose that house, but the mortgage meant that was always hanging over our heads. We did everything we could to pay off early: a little extra every month, a one time payment every once in a while. The feeling of relief and freedom when we paid the last dollar was unanticipated in its intensity, and amazing in its freeing effect. Once you cross the line from slavery to freedom, you never want to go back, and you want to help others cross too.

AN EXAMPLE OF DEBT SLAVERY

Most people unfortunately have the experience of being enslaved to debt. I want to put some numbers and specifics in front of you, so everyone can see how the chains get forged, and how to break them.

Example:

Let's look at Bob's finances, and how he sold himself into slavery. Bob is a recent college graduate, with pretty average finances:

Annual salary $44,000

Student loan balance $27,000, 5% interest, 25 year term

Car loan balance $10,000, 10% interest, 5 year term

Total credit card balance $16,000, 18% interest, 25 year payoff

Home mortgage $100,000, 6% interest, 30 year term

I know that Bob's numbers are not your numbers. We'll work through Bob's example anyway. Feel free to change the example to your numbers, and work through it again. This isn't meant to be **Bob's** recipe for **your** financial success, but Bob's **example** that you can use to learn.

Bob has to pay about $1,230 every month to stay current on his debts, about one third of his income. He is enslaved by $153,000 of total debt, or three and a half years of his total income. Since we're only looking at the debt side of his finances, we don't know whether he is making ends meet, although the unpaid credit card balance suggests that he's spent past his income in months past.

The debt load means that twenty years from now Bob will still be paying for things that he bought today. He has one third of everything he earns already committed. He has $153,000 standing between him and any decision – a new career, a new ministry, a new business opportunity, a new purchase. In an age of freedom and self-expression, he has already committed one third of his freedom for 25 years to expressions he's already made.

The point of the example, though, is not to highlight the problems of debt. We can take Solomon's word for it, and, if you labor under the cloud of debt, you already know it. The point is to caution against debt, and to give us some numbers to work with as we discuss how to get out of debt.

BREAKING THE CHAINS OF DEBT

There are several steps to getting out of debt, and you need to take them in order.

Step 1. Stop digging.

The first step of getting out of a hole is to stop digging the hole deeper. You have to make the commitment that you are not going to borrow any more money. New purchases on your credit cards are going to be paid in full, or better, you are going to pay cash for everything.

But what about unplanned expenses? Medical bills, or car repairs? We'll talk more about those when we look at Solomon's advice about planning ahead and about spending wisely, but for now just look at the mind game being played here. The admonition is to pay cash for all your expenses. The rejoinder tries to focus attention on undefined, unplanned expenses, and use that as a counterargument to paying cash for everything else. If you have to be enslaved for a time to cover unexpected medical bills, so be it. But don't use the possibility of something unexpected in the future as an argument to keep you from managing what you can plan today. Don't let a hypothetical exception keep you from getting the benefit of the rule.

The other steps in the chain-breaking process will improve your financial condition, which will make people much more willing to lend you money. If you don't start with a firm commitment that you are not going to borrow any more money, then the lure of easy money will make it very easy to slide back into slavery.

It can be surprising what you can do once you make that commitment. At one time, our dining room table was a picnic table I built, and we sat on benches plus one rocking chair. We had committed to paying cash for any new furniture, and sitting on benches didn't hurt us a bit. Guests probably found it a bit unusual, but we didn't want to be enslaved to debt just so we could lie to guests about what furniture we could afford. Keeping that commitment in small things made it easier to keep it in large things, and enabled us to get free of debt.

Step 2. Get some operating margin.

The money you have in your budget that is not already marked for specific expenses is your operating margin. If you spend every dollar you make, then you are not going to be able to do anything about your debt. You have to get some operating margin to work with.

Success at Step 1 (stop digging) should bring your monthly finances to zero net – you spend only what you bring in. In Step 2 you have to spend a little less than you bring in. There are many ways to do this, depending on your situation. We'll go into a more detail when we talk about spending wisely, but consider just a few ideas here. Can you eat at home a little more instead of restaurants? If you must eat out, can you skip the soda and alcohol, and drink water instead? Do you really need premium cable or satellite TV? Can you raise/lower your thermostat a little?

Bringing in a little more than you spend can also give you some margin. Can you work a few more hours? Can you qualify for bonuses? Can you sell stuff you don't use? Is there part time work available?

To get out of debt, you have to pay it off. So you have to have some money to work with.

Step 3. Be the Chief Financial Officer of your debt.

Incurring debt is usually an asset question – you want something (hopefully an asset, but maybe just entertainment), and you borrow money to buy it. In Step 1 you've already committed to stop borrowing money.

Paying off debt is a math question. The fun part of acquiring the asset is done, what is left is the math of the payoff. You have balances, interest rates, terms, etc. on various debts. You have to work out the numbers so you get the balances to zero. You're defeating the evil monster in a computer game. Your debt balance is the monster, and your weapon is your operating margin. The strategy you use to get the most out of your weapon is the math problem. Like the Chief Financial Officer of a company, you have to work the numbers to make the dollars add up in the most efficient way possible, and then tell the operating parts of the company (you when you buy things or earn money) the boundaries.

I encourage you to take the time to really understand how your debts work, how each interest charge and each payment affect the balance. Let's take a very simple example as an illustration: $1,000 loan, at 1% per month.

Here's what happens if you pay $40 per month:

month	interest	payment	balance
0	-	0	1,000.00
1	10.00	40	970.00
2	9.70	40	939.70
3	9.40	40	909.10

...

27	1.14	40	75.37
28	0.75	40	36.13
29	0.36	40	(3.51)

The full debt is paid off in 29 months.

Now, look at what happens if you pay an extra $20 per month:

month	interest	payment	balance
0	-	0	1,000.00
1	10.00	60	950.00
2	9.50	60	899.50
3	9.00	60	848.50

...

month	interest	payment	balance
16	1.95	60	137.11
17	1.37	60	78.48
18	0.78	60	19.26

At $60 per month, the debt is paid off in just 18 months. Almost a full year sooner. Anything you can add to the payment each month helps.

What if you could renegotiate the interest rate to just 0.5% per month?

month	interest	payment	balance
0	-	0	1,000.00
1	5.00	40	965.00
2	4.83	40	929.83
3	4.65	40	894.47

...

month	interest	payment	balance
25	0.55	40	70.43
26	0.35	40	30.78
27	0.15	40	(9.06)

You cut about 2 months off the end of the payment stream. It's probably worth doing, but does not have as big an effect.

The biggest input to your debt math problem is the amount you owe. The other two inputs to your debt math problem are

34

the payment you make and the interest rate you pay. Becoming the Chief Financial Officer of your debt means that you look at each debt you have, and make a plan for reducing those inputs however you can. I kept spreadsheets on each of our debts, and could see the effect of making any extra payments. I would calculate how much I would have to add to this month's payment to cut off one month from the total term, or how much sooner we'd pay off if we could add just $10 per month to the payment. It's easier to prioritize debt payments if you can see the effects. There are lots of tools available to help you with this. A step by step guide to building spreadsheets like the ones I used is in an appendix to this book.

Do the math before you make trades, though – a closing cost or loan origination fee can cost you more than a lower interest rate saves. It depends on your debt, but once you have some monthly margin to work with, you may be able to renegotiate some of your debts. A payment today is risk free for a lender, so requests to renegotiate that are connected to offers to pay something today are more likely to succeed. A warning, though – be sure you do the math and know that the renegotiation will really be a net win, and do not succumb to the temptation to take on more debt (higher principal) as part of any renegotiation. Remember to include closing costs, or processing fees, or any other payment or obligation that is part of the deal.

Step 4. Start cutting links off your chains.

Once you have a commitment to no new debt, and some operating margin to work with, and understanding of just how your debt math problem works, then you can start using your margin to cutting links off your chains.

There are several ways to apply your margin.

Put all of your margin against the debt with the highest interest rate. This approach pays off the most expensive (in terms of interest) debt first, and is the mathematically optimal approach for solving the debt math problem. If the highest interest rate debt has a large principal, then you may spend a long time paying that debt while several smaller debts are still plodding along.

Spread your margin across all your debts. You just divide up your margin among all your debts, and pay a little extra on each. Like any approach that pays principal faster, this will work. I think the other approaches give better motivational feedback, though.

Put all of your margin against the debt that most enslaves you. Select this approach if there is a particular debt that has the biggest psychological impact on you. For example, if you've borrowed from a family member, the unpaid debt might be a big strain on that relationship. Paying that off first might have the highest "freedom" impact. Or if you are really stressed about losing your car if you default, then paying off the car loan might be the highest priority. If they are recourse debts, then a default on any one could put any of your assets at risk, so the "freedom" benefit is psychological more than real, but your motivation to continue the process is important.

Put all of your margin against the debt with the smallest balance. This approach ignores the cost of interest, but puts you on the shortest path to a success event, to dropping the first link off your debt chain. Getting free of debt can be a multiyear process, and it is important to experience success along the way. Each debt you close out strengthens your resolve to continue.

Which approach you take depends on who you are, what motivates you, and your particular debts. The highest interest rate debts often have the smallest balances – house and car loans are usually higher balances and lower interest rates than consumer loans and credit cards, so paying off small balances and paying off high interest rates are often the same thing.

I personally need to experience incremental success in long projects, so we paid off small balance debts first. We'd use all of our margin on just one debt, and only pay the minimum required on all the other debts. The targeted debt would get its minimum payment plus all of our operating margin each month, plus any unexpected cash. Then, when that debt was eliminated, its former minimum payment would become an addition to our operating margin. We could use a little of that newly increased margin to celebrate our success, and then apply the rest to the next debt targeted. By the time we were going after our biggest debts, we had our original margin, plus all the other payments we used to have to make, to use against it.

Let's go back to Bob, and help him get free of debt using the smallest balance first strategy. Bob understands the seriousness of his debt slavery, and has arranged his personal finances to get $400 per month margin to use against his debt chains. This is about 10% of his income – maybe he got a raise, or a part-time job, or cut his cable TV, skipped some fancy dinners out, or some combination of all those. This is what can happen when Bob puts that margin against his debt:

Bob's puts the entire $400 extra on his credit card debt, so he pays $643 per month on that debt. The whole $16,000 is paid off by month 31.

At month 31 Bob still owes $5,400 on his car loan, but now he puts the $643 that he was paying on the credit card against the car loan. That link in the chain falls quickly – with the extra payment, Bob pays the car off by month 38.

Now Bob has $856 of margin – the original $400, plus the $243 minimum credit card payment, plus the $213 car loan minimum payment. He adds that $856 to paying off the $25,300 he still owes on his student loan. Paying $1,030 instead of the $174 minimum lets him cut through that link in the chain by month 64.

Bob is on a roll. In just about 5 years, he has paid off all his debt except his house. He's even kept any raises or bonuses for his own celebration; rolling those into the debt freedom project would speed things up even more. Let's keep our eye on the ball, though, and have Bob roll the $1,030 he used to pay on the student loan into his attack on the $92,500 he still owes on his house. The house is paid off by month 130.

Take a minute to see what Bob has done. He took a one time step back in his lifestyle of about 10%. He increased his lifestyle from there in step with promotions and raises, but just kept it $400/month less than it could have been. In about eleven years, that small reduction has let him pay off $153,000 of debt. It has also set him free from all his debt almost 20 years earlier than scheduled. He how has no debt, and the $1,630 every month that he was paying against his house is now free to him.

Avoid debt in the first place. If you're already enslaved, avoid any more debt, and cut off the links of your debt chain as soon as you can.

DON'T TRY TO GET RICH QUICKLY, OR GET RICH BY CHEATING

Solomon's second principle is a warning against trying to get rich quickly, or to get rich by cheating. I've grouped these together since they are based on the same basic appeal – getting money without working for it.

A desire to get money without really working for it is common, and get rich quick schemes are designed to appeal to this. There is usually some work involved, but the promised rewards are far out of proportion to the work required. The appeal is that you get money without work. But that is not how money works. You get money when you provide something of value to someone else, usually by applying your time and effort to do something they want done. You work for them, they pay you money. Get rich quick schemes try to get money without providing value. They tempt you to focus on money (what you get), instead of the work to earn it (what you do). That's the wrong focus – who you are, and what you do, are far more important than how much stuff you have. Also, you can control what you do, but you can't control what you get.

Cheating to get money is based on the same appeal – getting money without working to provide value first. It's easier to see that it's wrong since there is an identifiable victim. We're talking about the person trying to get the money, though, and any approach that focuses on getting money without working has the same problem.

Getting rich involves more than working, but getting rich without work doesn't work. We know this is true, because the Bible says it and because experience confirms it. A few reminders from Solomon:

"Wealth obtained by fraud will dwindle, but whoever earns it through labor will multiply it." (Proverbs 13:11 HCSB).

"Making a fortune through a lying tongue is a vanishing mist, a pursuit of death." (Proverbs 21:6 HCSB).

"The righteousness of the upright will deliver them, But the treacherous will be caught by their own greed." (Proverbs 11:6 NASB).

"Bread obtained by falsehood is sweet to a man, But afterward his mouth will be filled with gravel." (Proverbs 20:17 NASB).

"But he who makes haste to be rich will not go unpunished." (Proverbs 28:20 NASB).

As we noted earlier, big winners of lotteries win, on average, more than enough to pay off all their current debt. But lottery winners are about twice as likely to file for bankruptcy as others. Callie Rogers blew a 2003 U.K. lottery jackpot of $3 million on shopping, cocaine, friends, and breast augmentation and told reporters she was working as a maid. William "Bud" Post squandered his 1988 Pennsylvania prize of more than $16 million on houses, vehicles and bad businesses before going bankrupt. He served time for firing a shotgun at a bill collector before his death in 2006.

Trying to get rich by cheating doesn't hurt just the cheater: "The one who profits dishonestly troubles his household". Proverbs 15:27 HCSB). Bernie Madoff ran a Ponzi scheme, and was one of the richest men in New York. He ultimately stole about $65billion. That's a lot of wealth "obtained by falsehood." Bernie was sentenced to a 150 year prison sentence. The shame brought on his family led his son to suicide, and Bernie acknowledges that he caused his son's suicide. Families who tried to get rich quick with Madoff lost everything. Charities who tried to multiply their money through Madoff's fraud had to cease operations. The people who tried to get rich quick with Madoff's schemes all lost; Madoff, trying to get rich by cheating, lost all.

WHY DO PEOPLE TRY?

The basic appeal here is like the first temptation in the Garden of Eden: the serpent told Eve she could be like God. We feel a constant pull to try to put ourselves in charge of the universe. We have to work for what we want – God said it, and that's the way the world works. But we don't like that rule. We'd rather be God, and tell the universe what to do. We want the universe to provide for our comforts just because we want them.

The bait in the trap is money without work. All we have to do is sacrifice our character, the part that tells us that it's wrong to take something from another person without giving something in return. The sad thing about the trap is that, even if we could trade comforts for character, we don't really want to.

We don't want to be worthless, comfortable people. We want to be heroes. Heroes are not those who found an easy or dishonest way to get wealth. Heroes face challenges, persist through adversity, and keep working even when things seem bleak. When heroes get rewards, we cheer them because we know the rewards are well-earned. I'd rather be a man I respect, than be physically comfortable but disgusted with myself.

HOW TO AVOID THE TRAP IN YOUR LIFE

I have read that, in an emergency situation while driving a car, you should focus on where you want to go, and not on where you don't want to go. If you are in danger of hitting another car, don't look at the other car; look at the space you want to drive into instead. I think it is the same with avoiding the temptations to get rich by cheating.

Appeals to get rich quickly, and opportunities to get money by cheating, surround us. I am not sure you can even recognize every one. To avoid them, don't look at them. Instead of focusing on the temptations, focus on strengthening your character, particularly the part that reminds you to work for what you want. Strengthening your character, just like strengthening your body, takes steady incremental effort. Exercise with light weights, or run short distances, to build your ability to take on heavier weights or longer distances. Look for small chances to be honest in getting money, for small chances to avoid cheating, so that you will be strong enough to resist bigger temptations.

Remember that big things are made of little things. A big character is made of lots of small acts. The strength to resist big temptations is developed by resisting little temptations. This is true of all aspects of your character, including building the strength to resist cheating. We have to look for every opportunity to resist the temptation to cheat. These temptations come at us from all different directions: games that don't really count for anything, office supplies that come home from work, shortcuts taken in hobbies, applying less than your best at work, playing lotteries or other forms of gambling, accepting more than the correct change at a store. As you find, and root out, these failings, you will become more sensitive to them and be able to recognize and avoid the traps before you fall into them.

Some of these shortcuts may seem like no big deal – it's just a little money. No one will miss a dime. It may be true that all you are costing the other person is a negligible amount of money. But then all you are getting is a negligible amount of money, money that God and experience promise you will not keep anyway. The real cost is not the little money gained or lost; the real cost is that you've just made yourself smaller. You've just cut out part of your character, part of who you are. Being sure of your own character is far more valuable than a little money that you won't keep anyway.

DON'T BE LAZY

Solomon's third warning is against laziness. There's a lot we could say about being lazy, but for now we need to just focus on what laziness has to do with money.

Remember that money is not the goal – it is an intermediate form of translating what you do to the outcome you want (hopefully, to an outcome in line with God's will). There are other routes to translate your actions to outcomes – you might be in school, or managing a household, or raising kids, or growing a garden, or any number of other life activities. Those are all valuable; my focus on money here is not meant to downgrade or demean any of those. Avoiding laziness applies to those activities, as well, but we're looking at just money here.

Let's look again at some verses warning against laziness:

"Do not love sleep, or you will become poor; Open your eyes, and you will be satisfied with food." (Proverbs 20:13 NASB).

"A little sleep, a little slumber, a little folding of the arms to rest, and your poverty will come like a robber, your need, like a bandit." (Proverbs 24:33 HCSB).

"The sluggard does not plow after the autumn, So he begs during the harvest and has nothing." (Proverbs 20:4 NASB).

It seems like a little laziness can't hurt much. Surely everyone deserves a little rest and relaxation, right? I guess so, but we should keep in mind the consequences that follow laziness, and take that question with appropriate seriousness. Proverbs 24:33 warns us that just a "little slumber" leads to poverty coming like a robber. A robber doesn't give any advance warning. You are moving right along, not suspecting anything, and then the bandit shows up and takes all your money.

The temptation of laziness leads us to be a little lazy today, and a little more lazy tomorrow. Proverbs 26:15 gives us the picture of a slacker, who eventually gets too lazy to even feed himself: "The slacker buries his hand in the bowl; he is too weary to bring it to his mouth." (Proverbs 26:15 HCSB). We start to define our laziness today in comparison to our laziness yesterday – it doesn't take long until compound interest on our laziness overwhelms us. At first nothing seems amiss, but then it eventually catches up to you and your poverty comes like a robber.

But does that mean that you have to always be working? Slave away to make as much money as you can? Of course not. Solomon also warns us that the pursuit of money is not what your life should be about. Even Solomon's warnings about laziness don't expressly command you to work for money. They just tell you that if you're lazy you will be poor.

Your life is made of what you spend your time on. You have 24 hours every day, and your life is made by what you get in trade for those hours. TV and movies are fun and popular, but would you rather watch someone else live, or live yourself? Computer games are thrilling, but would you rather act in a pretend, computer-simulated world or in the real world? Keeping up with friends on-line is a great way to stay in touch, but how much time do you want to spend keeping track of what someone's cat had for breakfast?

I'm not saying that those things are inherently evil, or that you are wrong to enjoy them. I am saying, along with Solomon, that you need to be careful about whether those things are leading you into what Solomon would call laziness. They apparently are for many in the U.S. A few numbers from the U.S. Bureau of Labor Statistics (http://www.bls.gov/news.release/atus.t11.htm), and their implications:

Men spend an average of 21.41 hours per week watching TV. That is the equivalent of a half-time job. Recall the earlier example of getting Bob out of debt – putting just 10% of his lifestyle expenses into debt repayment got Bob out of debt in 10 years instead of 30. If Bob worked an extra 20 hours per week, instead of watching TV, he would be out of debt in just 5 years. 30 years of debt slavery gone in just 5 years! That doesn't mean that you can't watch TV, but realize that those idle hours cost a lot. Would you work instead of watch TV for five years to be debt free for the rest of your life?

As another comparison, it is estimated that basic competency in a new language takes 200-300 hours (there's a lot of variability in that, but just take the figure as a comparison point). Learning a new language would take just 10-15 weeks of the average American's TV time.

Another one: a modest home can be built, from start to finish, with about 1,000 man hours. That's less than one year of average TV time. Would you give up TV for a year to move into a new house?

The point here is not that you can't watch TV, or interact online, or take naps. The point is that those activities have a cost. A lot of people are dissatisfied with their economic position. A lot of people think that God hasn't blessed them with the money they need to live. But God already warned us, through Solomon, that being idle leads to poverty. You can trade your life for TV and movies and video games and social media, but don't complain when your poverty comes on you like a bandit.

My examples were mostly centered on money, but the principle goes to other activities, too. Being lazy in any activity means becoming poor in that activity. If you're lazy in managing a household, then your household will be poorly managed. If you're lazy in learning at school, then you will be poorly educated.

The tragedy of laziness, like most temptations to live contrary to God's teaching, is that you end up making a losing trade. Being lazy is trading your life and getting nothing in return. That is the same as destroying it. "The one who is truly lazy in his work is brother to a vandal." (Proverbs 18:9).

What is worth trading for your life? Minute by minute, you trade the time of your life for things that make you a better person (more like what God and you want you to be), or things that make the world a better place (more in line with what God and you want it to be), or both. Even sleeping when you're tired makes you a better person, since it prepares you for the next day. But what does laziness do to that trade? You trade your life for something that does not make you a better person, and does not make the world a better place. You are essentially practicing being dead. Like Solomon says, don't do that.

Now you know what not to do, it's time to talk about what to do instead.

PLAN AHEAD

We've gone through Solomon's "do nots" – do not go into debt, do not cheat, do not be lazy. These are critical, but focusing on the "do nots" is not enough to get you to the financial position you want. It is very hard to stop a bad habit unless at the same time you replace it with a good habit. We see this in experience – if you dwell on a bad habit, you never get rid of it. We also see it in Solomon's advice, where most of the "do not do this" warnings have a companion "do this instead" encouragement.

The next three in Solomon's list are the positive things to do. They roughly correspond to the three "do nots" (although I juggled the order): don't go into debt, but plan ahead instead; don't try to get rich quick, but use your money wisely; and don't be lazy, but work.

We already practiced planning ahead in the section on debt, where part of the key to getting out of debt is to plan how you are going to pay debt off. In this section, I want to present some more thinking points about planning ahead.

THE ACT OF PLANNING HAS A POWERFUL EFFECT ON YOU

Our emotions often drive what we do. Our emotions give us the motivation and energy to do things. Many times our emotions seem to be in control, and that can be a good thing. You don't want to spend a lot of time planning how to evade a bus that is about to hit you. You want to act right away. The same immediate emotional response, however, can lead you into impulse purchases or other bad financial moves.

While your emotions at the moment can overwhelm rational thinking, over time your conscious thought can train your emotions. When you plan, you set your conscious mind to work on envisioning a future, and rehearsing the steps necessary to get there. Those thoughts gradually train your emotions, so that the subconscious parts of your brain start cooperating with your conscious plan. I am simplifying a lot of neuroscience here, but the basic idea is widely recognized in concepts as diverse as "managing with the end in mind" and "think and grow rich."

Further, one of our strongest drives as people is to make our reality be consistent with our words. We try very hard to tell the truth so that our words match reality, and to live out what we say so that reality matches our words. Even when we don't, we try to rationalize the disconnect. Once you have articulated a plan, or a desired outcome, then your built-in desire to make reality conform to your words will help drive you toward your goal.

PLANS FAIL, BUT PLAN ANYWAY

We've all experienced something that didn't go according to plan. We know that we can't plan for everything that might happen, and our plans are always lagging behind the real world. There is even an acronym for it: OBE, meaning Overtaken By Events, as an explanation for why a planned action was not taken. Or, as Helmuth von Moltke the Elder said "No plan survives contact with the enemy" (obviously an old quote, since no one names their child Helmuth any more).

If you can't count on your plans, then why bother to make them? Because the act of planning is essential to training your mind and your emotions to be ready to act in the direction you want to go. General Dwight Eisenhower said "Plans are nothing; planning is everything." What did he mean?

Planning teaches your mind what to look for, how to react, and what is important to decisions. So when reality shows up different than in your plan, you already know the basic direction you want to go, and you have practiced making decisions and trades. Adjusting a plan is much easier than making one up on the fly, or flying blind.

WHAT SOLOMON SAYS ABOUT PLANNING AHEAD

Solomon tells us to figure out how to provide for you and your family. Do things at the right time – gather provisions when they are available.

"Go to the ant, O sluggard, Observe her ways and be wise, Which, having no chief, Officer or ruler, Prepares her food in the summer And gathers her provision in the harvest." (Proverbs 6:6-8 NASB).

Plan for provision before luxury. Planning for luxuries is ok, but plan for provision first.

"Prepare your work outside And make it ready for yourself in the field; Afterwards, then, build your house." (Proverbs 24:27 NASB).

Before every airplane flight, you are advised, in the event of an emergency, to put on your own oxygen mask first and then to help those who need help. You have to take care of the things that are essential for survival, then you will have time (or money) to spend on the rest.

As important as planning is, planning by itself is not enough. You have to do what you plan. You have to be diligent in carrying out the plan, which means that your plan has to match the realities of your capabilities and the reality around you. Solomon said it like this:

"The plans of the diligent lead surely to advantage, But everyone who is hasty comes surely to poverty." (Proverbs 21:5 NASB).

HOW DO YOU PLAN?

You are probably already a good planner, at least in some areas of your life. You just have to recognize those skills, and apply them to your dealings with money.

What do you have to have to make a plan? You have to know the starting point, the destination, the timing, and the constraints. As a simple exercise, let's look at a simple plan for going out to eat.

Starting point. We might be starting from our home, or work, or a hotel if we're traveling, or a theater if we went to a movie first. The plan has to start at the right place. The starting point also includes things that are in your control that affect your plan. For example, you might have to own a tuxedo if Joe's Bar and Grill is a very formal place, or an umbrella if it's raining and Joe's is an outdoor place.

Destination. "Where do you want to go?" We have to have an answer for this before our plan makes any sense. You can't plan "let's go eat somewhere"; you can plan "Let's go to Joe's Bar and Grill."

Timing. When can we start, and how much time do we have to get there? Joe's Bar and Grill might be a pleasant one hour walk, but that won't work if we have to be there in 15 minutes.

Constraints. These have to do with things about the world that we don't control but that we have to consider in our plan. For example, our favorite route to Joe's might be closed for construction. Or Joe's might be closed on Tuesdays.

This might seem too simple, but it's often good to check your skills on easy tasks, before applying them to hard ones. Walk before you run, or practice before you play the real game. Now let's apply these foundational planning skills to money in your life.

PLANNING AHEAD IN MONEY MATTERS

There is a lot of good advice about budgeting, but often people don't want to budget because they don't want to accept limits on their spending. This is a wrong perspective on budgets, and prevents people from enjoying the freedom that a budget gives you – that's right, a budget gives you **freedom**.

You already have limits on your spending – you can't spend more than you have, earn, and can borrow. A budget doesn't add any new limits; it just puts you in charge of how those limits affect you. A budget is simply a way of planning how you are going to spend your money. A budget gives you the freedom to make decisions about where you will spend your money, instead of always making decisions when your balance is almost zero, and being a hostage to the needs of the moment. A budget is part of your financial plan, but only part. And, like all plans, budgets don't survive first contact with the enemy. The process of making the plan is the critical part, so filling numbers into someone else's preplanned budget worksheet doesn't help that much – it gives you **a** plan, but it's not **your** plan, so you've missed most of the value. I encourage you to use the planning tools you already use every day, like those we talked about above, to make an overall money plan. Then your budget planning grows out of that, and the fact that you understood the plan makes it more likely that it will be useful to you.

Starting point. Think about where you are right now, in whatever dimension you are planning about. Since we're talking about money, think about where you are in terms of money. What skills do you have that people will pay you for? What is your monthly income? What is your bank balance? How much debt do you have? Are you stuck in a get rich quick scheme? Are you lazy?

Destination. Where do you want to go? What is your vision for your future? You probably have several levels of destination to think about. You want to get out of all debt, but maybe you first need a destination of not going any further into debt, then paying off credit card debt. Your destination might include buying a car or a house or a business. It might include finishing a degree. It might include saving to help your kids pay for college. It should include things like being able to pay for unexpected car or house repairs without borrowing money. I hope the destination for your life includes a lot more than these money topics, but you need to have some money destinations in mind if you are to get enough control of your money that you use money as a tool to get where else you are going.

Timing. A goal without a date is just a wish. Think about the timing of each of your destinations. Be aggressive, but not unrealistic. Our man Bob took several years to buy his way out of debt slavery. Set delivery dates for the monetary goals that are important for you. You might have to refigure these as you plan, and as reality affects your plan, but acknowledging that you have a goal, and having a date to reach that goal, establishes the basis for your plan and gives you the motivation to succeed. Most people work harder when facing a deadline, and beating your deadline for a money goal is a huge ego boost.

Constraints. What things in your life affect your money situation but are not in your direct control? You may have children's expenses to cover, or an elderly parent, or special medical needs. You may have already committed to finish a degree. Maybe you can't get a million dollar signing bonus because you are not athletic enough for pro sports. Maybe you must keep a car so you can get to work. Think about what external boundaries will affect your finances, so that you don't plan a route through solid walls or over impassable terrain.

The plan. Now that you know where you're starting from and what you're starting with, where you're going, how long you have to get there, and what obstacles you have to avoid, the hardest parts of the plan are mostly done. In one sense, you already have a plan – it's a one step plan, jumping direct from starting point to destination.

If your destinations are at all ambitious, however, you probably need smaller steps to put together to reach your destination. Each step needs to be something specific that you can do. When we got Bob free from debt, he had specific steps in his freedom plan – reduce expenses, pay smallest balance, roll over payments to next smallest balance, and so on. If you need to buy a new car: how much does the car you need cost? How are you going to get the operating margin to begin saving for the purchase price? Where are you going to invest your savings, and at what rate of return? How long will that take? If the required time is too long, then how are you going to get more operating margin?

Destinations that are closer to your starting point are probably easier to plan, while those that are farther away may require you to consider big steps. Do you need to change careers? Do you need to move to a less expensive house? Or less expensive city? Free your mind at the planning stage. Some bad decisions are very costly in real life, but they are free when you're planning.

What if you sold the extra car? Could your family still get around town? How much money would you add to your margin – payment, gas, insurance, repairs? What would that do to your plan? Maybe being crimped on transportation for a couple of years is worth paying off some particularly unpleasant debt early.

What if your spouse quit work to stay at home with the kids? What would you lose in income? What would you save on transportation, clothes, meals out, home repair? What would you lose or gain in non-monetary areas of your life?

These kinds of decisions can be hard to make in real life, and even harder to un-make. But you can make and un-make them easily while you're planning. When you buy clothes, you try them on to be sure that you'll like them when they are part of your life. Similarly when you're planning – try on lots of scenarios, and do the math to see what effect they have on your outcomes. You will not pick most of them (you often can't pick more than one – you can't both sell and not sell the extra car!), but the process of thinking about them helps you understand your priorities, the costs and benefits of various possible decisions. This is why planning can be more important than plans; you train your mind to recognize tradeoffs, and you are not caught unprepared by opportunities or setbacks.

One other step that I find useful, but my wife finds annoying, when I make plans: once I'm pretty happy with a plan, I often try to test the boundaries. I look at all the minor variations that are possible in my starting point, destination, timing, and constraints. What if I got a raise? What if the price went up? What if we wanted to pay the debt off one month sooner? Often this doesn't result in any change to the plan, but sometimes if reveals a good variation on the plan. At the very least, I have the benefit of planning for variations, so when variations happen (as they always do), I am prepared.

Sometimes (and this gets really annoying to my wife) I even try major variations to test my assumptions. I look at the things that we assumed were unchangeable assumptions in the plan, and think about what would happen if we changed them. What if we moved from our house in the country to an apartment in a big city? What if we changed careers? What if we decided to go out for Thanksgiving dinner instead of cook it at home? Or buy a turkey chick and grow our own dinner? Most often, this process leads to absurd, and sometimes funny, results. But sometimes it reveals an important opportunity, and at least it helps insulate us against doubt when tougher times come.

Bottom line – plan ahead, and don't be afraid to second guess yourself **while you're planning**. Once you've made the plan, then be diligent about it, but remember that every plan gets overtaken by events. The work you did in planning lets you overcome when your plan gets overtaken.

WORK

This is the counterpart to "don't be lazy." The advice to work also comes with a promise: if you work, then you will have enough. If you want things, and don't want to work, then you are prime prey for the trap of trying to get rich quick or by cheating, or for being enslaved by debt. If you want things, and do work, then God promises that you will have enough.

Benefiting from Solomon's advice about work is a matter of attitude before it is a matter of detailed instruction. Solomon probably did not know how to do your job as well as you already do. In fact, you almost certainly do your job better than most of the people in the world could do your job (since most of the people in the world do some other job). But your perspective on work can make all the difference in whether you are confident and at peace about your work, or dread it and worry about it. So we will focus on a few important attitudes about work, and see how Solomon's advice helps us have the right perspective on work.

Before we start, let's get Solomon's words on work fresh in mind:

"The Lord will not allow the righteous to hunger, But He will reject the craving of the wicked. Poor is he who works with a negligent hand, But the hand of the diligent makes rich. He who gathers in summer is a son who acts wisely, But he who sleeps in harvest is a son who acts shamefully." (Proverbs 10:3-5 NASB).

"He who tills his land will have plenty of bread, But he who pursues worthless things lacks sense." (Proverbs 12:11 NASB).

"The hand of the diligent will rule, But the slack hand will be put to forced labor." (Proverbs 12:24 NASB).

"In all labor there is profit, But mere talk leads only to poverty." (Proverbs 14:23 NASB).

WORK IS GOOD, NOT EVIL

Work is often seen as a necessary evil, something bad that we have to endure because we toil in this fallen world. The Garden of Eden must have been so nice, with perfect weather and no work. But that's not how the story goes. Whether you believe Genesis is literal or only an illustration, God gave Adam work to do before Adam sinned: "God blessed them, and God said to them, "Be fruitful, multiply, fill the earth, and subdue it. Rule the fish of the sea, the birds of the sky, and every creature that crawls on the earth." (Genesis 1:28 HCSB). Work is part of being human, and was part of being human before there was any evil in the picture.

Do you begrudge going to work? Maybe you have a demanding job, or have to work long hours. Some work is tiring, and some bosses are hard to work for, and it's fine to acknowledge those things. But you should also realize that you are going to trade the minutes of your life today for something. You can trade them for idleness – be lazy, and have the assurance of poverty. Or you can trade them for entertainment – still sort of lazy, and you will be poor. Or you can trade them for something productive – that's the definition of work. Isn't your life worth trading for productive activities? Realize that you **want** to work. You might need to think about where you work, or what kind of work you do, but the idea of work is good.

Keep this perspective, then, when you think about the drawbacks to your job. Realize that you are going to work, and so your concerns should not be about going to work. Your concerns should be about whether this job is the most productive trade you can make for your time. If not, then keep working, but also work to make a better trade – more education, a different company, better tools, whatever will help your work be more productive. The question of where you work, or what you do as work, implicates the planning principles we discussed earlier. What skills do you have now? What skills could you develop? What is the outcome you want from your work (money, and what else? Free time? Work outdoors? Prestige?)? If you need to make changes, what is the path from where you are today to where you want to be?

IF YOU WORK, YOU HAVE ENOUGH MONEY

Almost everyone wants a raise. Almost everyone thinks they deserve to be paid more. Budgets are tight, and if you just got paid a little more then things would be easy. Do you see yourself in that?

You might actually be underpaid, meaning that you produce more than you get paid for producing. Lay that question aside until you own the right attitude about whether you have enough money. In particular, you have to break out of the trap of focusing on how much you get paid.

Think about the statement "I have enough money." Whether this statement is true depends more on you than it depends on how much money you have. You earn some money, and spend some money. If you spend no more than you earn, then you have enough money. Whether you have enough money depends on how your spending compares with your income. It doesn't matter how much you earn. The news is full of people who earned millions of dollars and still went bankrupt. The news is not full of the millions of people who earn way less than millions of dollars, but stay solvent.

Solomon tells us that if you work, you will have enough to eat. He doesn't promise that you will have enough to eventually ignore his advice and quit working. He doesn't promise that you will have so much that you can buy boats in the desert. He does promise that you will have **enough**. The vital attitude adjustment is to stop the stress, and stop the complaining, about whether you have enough. You work, you earn, and then you manage what money you have. You can know it will be enough. If it's not enough, then you need to reassess your needs and your management, not grumble about being underpaid.

This is way out of line with what we're usually told. But in my experience it is amazingly freeing. There is a time to think about how much you are paid – when you are setting prices for your business, or negotiating for a new job, or deciding whether to get some new skill. But those are different from the actual work. Separate the worry over how much you are paid from the joy of the work itself, and both will go better.

UNDERPAID? UNAPPRECIATED? IT WILL CHANGE

But what if you really are underpaid? This is such a tempting excuse that it's worth analyzing in light of what Solomon told us about work. Why do you think you are not paid enough? Is it because you produce more than you are paid for? Or is it just because you think you need more money? If you just want more money, though, then remember that Solomon promises that you will have enough. So, however much money you have from working, it is by definition "enough."

Giving up the "I hate work" attitude is likely to lead you to be better at your work. If that's not recognized by your employer, then you may end up being really underpaid. What should you do?

Solomon has a promise here, too.

"Do you see a man skilled in his work? He will stand before kings; He will not stand before obscure men." (Proverbs 22:29 NASB).

Have you ever been frustrated at work? Your boss just doesn't appreciate you? Have you ever lost a job? Solomon tells us that our focus needs to be on being skilled in our work, not on the person evaluating us. If you are skilled in your work, God promises that you will stand before kings. That boss who doesn't see your skill must be one of the "obscure men" Solomon mentions. Make sure you're skilled, and not just grumpy. Solomon, as a king and as an employer of many thousands of men, must have been always on the lookout for men who were skilled in the work. There are far more opportunities looking for skilled workers than there are skilled workers looking for opportunities.

In your personal career, focus first on your attitude about work. If you have somewhere to work, focus first on having a thankful and content attitude. Next, manage the money you have according to Solomon's other principles instead of complaining about how little you are paid. Once your work attitude and money management are correct, then focus on being skilled in your work. After that you can check with Solomon's "kings" to see if you are ready to stand before them.

Look at your resume and think about whether you would pay your own money to hire yourself. Think about how your skills will make more money for an employer than the salary you want. What skills or experience do you need to add? How do you demonstrate tangible, reportable results on the quality of your work? What people, organizations, or employers do you need to meet, so they can see your quality? Maybe it's time to talk with your employer about what you produce and what you should be paid, and give your employer a chance to be a "king" instead of an "obscure man".

THE MYTH OF JOB SECURITY

Pursuing job security by finding or staying with a big company can tempt you to trust the big company for your financial position. The thought is that, if you work for a big, stable company, then you have your money needs covered and can avoid the hassle of managing your money, and your relationship with money, according to Solomon's principles.

This myth is dangerous on many fronts, and dispelling it is very important to taking control of your financial life. The more you rely on a company for security, the less you rely on the principles of Solomon. No company has the responsibility to provide for you; that responsibility is ultimately up to you. Companies and churches and friends can help, to be sure, but the responsibility is yours.

The myth of job security can make people stay in a job that is not "standing before kings." Jobs that might require changing companies, or using a different mix of skills, become unthinkable and even frightening since they call the big company security myth into question. But how can you stand before kings if you refuse to leave the barn? No matter how skilled you are in your work, you have to be willing to move to new opportunities if you are ever to become unstuck. Note that you might not have to **actually** move, but you have to be **willing** to move.

Your true job security comes from living your financial life according to Solomon's principles. The promise that you will have enough follows the command to work. Your job security comes from your ability and willingness to do something that other people will pay you for doing. That might be working for a large company, or a small company, or directly for customers.

Those who trust in large companies for security are primed for disaster, and too many have experienced it. Just in 2012, Hewlett-Packard cut 27,000 jobs, American Airlines cut 14,200 jobs, Lockheed Martin cut 10,000 jobs. These are huge companies, but that was no security for the fifty thousand workers laid off.

Like debt, trusting in a particular employer is a form of financial slavery. You must continue to work for that employer or your financial plans fail. That path does not lead to freedom; it slowly becomes ever more constraining. I had a co-worker once who was counting the days until retirement – he had just 14 **years** left. He was so tangled in a single company that he could not see that he was just counting the days until death. I wanted something more from my days, from my next 14 years. Taking to heart your personal responsibility for your own finances, and living based on that, can be scary at first but ultimately is exhilarating. Every step you take back from that responsibility is a step into financial slavery; every step you take into that responsibility is a step into freedom.

Your job security comes from the work you do, not from who you work for.

SPEND WISELY

It's pretty easy, and fun, to think of examples of other people not spending wisely. Racing heiress Tamara Ecclestone spent $1.5 million on a bathtub. Victoria Beckham spent $35,998 on a Stuart Hughes 24-carat cell phone. Pop star Lady Gaga spent $50,000 on an Electro-Magnetic Field Reader to keep ghosts at bay while she's on tour. NFL running back Arian Foster spent $70,000 to buy Segways (weight limit 260 pounds) for his offensive linemen (each of whom weighs over 300 pounds). That kind of spending leads many of the rich and famous into bankruptcy, which is easy to predict if you read Solomon's advice:

> "He who loves pleasure will become a poor man; He who loves wine and oil will not become rich." (Proverbs 21:17 NASB).
> "For the heavy drinker and the glutton will come to poverty, And drowsiness will clothe one with rags." (Proverbs 23:21 NASB).

While you may never make $200 million in a pro sports career, and then end up broke, those principles also apply to you. Getting control of your spending is the foundation of mastering your money, and is the prerequisite for getting out of debt. If you're interested enough in improving your finances to read this book, I hope that you've already cut out white tigers (Mike Tyson), zoos (Michael Jackson), and million dollar yachts (too many to list) from your spending. But there is much more to do, as always first in your attitude and then in your daily decisions.

"A penny saved is a penny earned" is an old saying often attributed to Benjamin Franklin. While there's truth in that statement, it actually falls rather far short of the mark. Let's look at what you have to do to put one additional penny in your pocket. Of course, you have to work to earn it. But to end up with one penny in your pocket, you have to do much more than one penny of work. You have to work enough additional to pay tax on the penny you eventually end up with: federal, state, local income tax, medicare and social security tax. You also have to work enough to cover your employer's expenses in employing you: payroll taxes, employer's share of social security tax, benefits. You also have to work enough to cover the expenses of doing your job: office supplies and space and furniture, tools, computers, etc. You also have to work enough to cover allowances for vacation and sick days. You also have to work enough to cover your share of the inefficiencies of office meetings, and complying with regulations, mandates, latest office policies, required training, etc. After all this, there still has to be some profit margin for your company. Even if you don't see all the expenses, or personally pay for them, they must be covered before that next penny reaches your pocket. All told, you have to work to produce many pennies before you end up with one of them in your pocket.

In contrast, once a penny is in your pocket, all you have to do to keep it there is not spend it. Which is a greater return on your effort? It is usually much easier to get margin for your financial plans by spending more wisely than by trying to earn more. Once you're spending wisely, earning more of course comes into play. The low hanging fruit, though, and the biggest return on your thinking time, is to figure out how to spend more wisely.

I don't know all of the items in your budget, so first let's look at a few principles when you're evaluating spending decisions.

Investment vs. Spending. Some spending temptations sound better when they are phrased as "investments." We are told that we are not spending money on something, but rather investing in the thing. This can be true, but take a hard, honest look at the decision before letting the phrasing influence you. An investment is money (or time) spent with the expectation of receiving a future return. As regards money, you should have a specific expectation and time table for return of the money invested, plus some increase, before you reclassify "spending money" as an "investment".

An energy efficiency upgrade to your home can be an investment if you have a specific plan for how much money it will save each month on utility bills. A time share vacation condo is only an investment if you have a specific plan to rent it out for more than you pay for it, or to spend a definite amount less on hotels because you are using the condo. Money investments that return non-money rewards are not investments – they are spending. They might be wise spending, but do not delude yourself into thinking of them as investments.

Quality vs. cost. The bitterness of poor quality is remembered long after the sweetness of low price has faded from memory. Consider with your purchases whether you need to have the low quality version of this item today, or can you wait to buy the high quality one later? Can you shuffle your spending so that you buy fewer, high quality items? If you buy low quality A and B today, you have A and B right now. But, in a few years, you have worn out A and B, and have to dispose of the worn out ones and have to buy them again. If you can buy high quality A today, though, and delay buying B until later, you may be able to spend the same total amount, have higher quality items, and not be faced with repairs or replacements as soon. Also, you will get to live with high quality possessions instead of a steady stream of low quality, wearing out things. But don't spend for quality that will not benefit you. Consider how often you will use something, how important performance is to you, how long you intend to use it, repair or maintenance costs, and the relative purchase prices. From another perspective, consider the total lifetime costs of an item, not just the today price in dollars.

Each family's spending decisions are unique, but see if you can be more wise in any of the following examples. They may not all be ingredients in your financial recipe, but take the ones that are useful, and apply the principles to your own life. This is only a starting point; there are many guides to saving money that are worth studying for ideas.

Eating out. Buying coffee at an expensive coffee shop each work day can run to $1,000 per year. Can you drink less? Or at less expensive places? Alcohol, or soft drinks, can add 10-50% to the cost of eating out. If eating out is a treat you can't give up, try drinking water and save at least that portion. Can you cut back on eating out? Eat at home more, or drop the restaurant desserts, or try less expensive places.

Entertainment. Cable TV prices have gone up four times the rate of inflation, and are commonly over $100 per month. Do you need all the premium channels? Do you need cable TV at all? We've been without cable TV for many years, and I love saving the money, and saving the time I would have spent watching it. We've used the savings to pay off debt, then to buy movies that we like to watch. Now we have more time, no debt, and a collection of movies to share with family and friends.

Transportation. How many cars do you have? How many do you need? Each car costs not just the cost of the car, but also fuel, maintenance, repairs, taxes, and insurance.

Recurring expenses. We all have expenses that regularly recur, and that seem like just part of life. Auto insurance, home insurance, and others. Check these every once in a while, and get competitive bids. The best value last year might not be the best value this year. Even with the same agent or company, ask about different policies or programs or discounts. Going to a higher deductible can save on many insurance policies; the risk of a higher deductible is not as much of a concern if you have some margin in your monthly budget.

Groceries. Are you shopping at the trendiest place or the place with the best value? A friend once called a local fashionable store the "Whole Paycheck Store" due to the high prices. Are you making the most of your grocery dollars, with warehouse stores, bulk purchases, coupons, seasonal sales, farmer's markets? Are you getting the best value, in terms of health and nutrition as well as price? Providing food is big business, with lots of suppliers competing for your dollars. Let them compete, and reward those that give you the best value by buying from them.

Clothing. Like groceries, this is a highly competitive industry. Prices and quality vary widely, and not always together. Buy clothes that you will wear, that will last, and shop for good prices. You have a wider range of options in clothing than almost anything else you buy, from list prices at posh stores to finding like-new clothes for pennies at resale shops.

Tools. By tools I mean conventional tools like hammers and drills, and also tools like computers and books and learning programs. Can you spend some of your time (like that saved by not watching as much TV) learning new skills? New skills that can help in your job, and new skills that can help you save money. Is there a tool that will help you do your work better or faster, or that will help you save money on repairs or help you make better buying decisions?

Housing. Are you in the right size house or apartment? Can you negotiate a lower rent, or refinance to lower your interest payment? What about utilities – can you turn off some lights, or replace them with low energy alternatives?

Education and activities. For you and your kids, take a hard look at the education and activity choices. Homeschool, private school, public school all have different costs and benefits. Remember to consider the impact on your life, though, since your goal of managing money better is to be able to manage life better. What about your activities? Would your family be better off, financially as well as relationally, if you hiked or played in the park together instead of paying for golf and playing on the most expensive sports team?

Church and charity. God has some specific things to say about contributing to the support of His work, and covering that requires that we bring in more than just Solomon's words. For now, though, consider whether you are supporting the ministries that are most in line with what God has called you to do. We've tried to pick a few ministries, and investigate them thoroughly, and then support them fully. It's hard to resist the many appeals for help that come your way, but it's very hard to be sure you are making wise giving decisions when you spread your support too many ways. You have an amount that you donate to church and charity; use your "spend wisely" tools in this area, too, to be sure your money is having the biggest impact.

As you get more control of your money life, spending wisely becomes more natural. It's a skill that you develop a little at a time, by constant practice. Each spending decision needs to be subject to this principle. Look to save dollars (the total cost of something), and percentages (since every penny counts). Don't get confused by false "investments" or by savings on something you didn't need (paying $100 for something that you don't need is a waste of $100, even if it's on sale, marked down from $200).

HOW DO YOU KNOW SOLOMON'S PRINCIPLES WILL WORK?

Who do you work for? Think of your employer, or your customers if you have your own business. You work for them, and they promise to pay you. Do you trust them to pay you what they promised? You must, or you would not keep working for them.

But, on another level, everyone works for God.

"The rich and the poor have a common bond, The Lord is the maker of them all." (Proverbs 22:2 NASB).

It's the same basic deal, though. You work the way God says, and He promises to pay you. He pays in money, and bread, and the other things you need for life. Do you trust Him? Has He paid His bills in the past? Have you had enough bread and money to live in the past? The answer must be yes or you would not be alive to read this.

Remember that money is an intermediate form for use in doing God's will. If you're doing God's will with the money you have, and you could do more if He gave you more money, then He has reason to give you more money.

But, if you're not doing what God wants with the money He's given you, why should He give you any more?

"Honor the Lord from your wealth, And from the first of all your produce; So your barns will be filled with plenty And your vats will overflow with new wine." (Proverbs 3:9-10 NASB).

"The generous man will be prosperous, And he who waters will himself be watered." (Proverbs 11:25 NASB).

"Why does a fool have money in his hand with no intention of buying wisdom?" (Proverbs 17:16 HCSB).

God wants you to honor Him by how you deal with money, He wants you to be generous in how you spend money, He wants you to manage your money to grow wise. If you are not doing those things, then God has little reason to trust you with money.

Even more importantly, remember that the intermediate form can never be the goal.

"Do not weary yourself to gain wealth, Cease from your consideration of it. When you set your eyes on it, it is gone. For wealth certainly makes itself wings Like an eagle that flies toward the heavens." (Proverbs 23:4-5 NASB).

It is certain - money will leave you. When it leaves you, and what you accomplish by it's leaving, are what matters.

So God tells us how to get money, but then says that we should not pursue it. What should we pursue instead? That's our next chapter.

MORE IMPORTANT THAN ALL -

LIVE WITH INTEGRITY

Solomon has one more principle, vital to understanding money but not really about how you get or spend money. It is about putting money in its place. Even though Solomon teaches us a lot about money, he tells us that integrity is more important.

"He who walks in integrity walks securely, But he who perverts his ways will be found out." (Proverbs 10:9 NASB)

"The integrity of the upright will guide them, But the crookedness of the treacherous will destroy them." (Proverbs 11:3 NASB).

I have had many business meetings with investors – people who managed and invested lots of money, in one case a half billion dollars of their family's money. The common theme of all the meetings was that the investors were looking for people with integrity. They were looking for deals with honest, trustworthy people. Venture capitalists look to invest in people – there are more good ideas and more good technologies than there are good people to work on them.

Solomon's six principles are all pretty much directly about money – how to get it, or keep it, or use it. Living with integrity does not seem to quite belong in a book about money, since it's not exactly about money. It's included for two reasons.

First, living with integrity makes every one of the six money principles easier to own and easier to live. Living with integrity includes paying your debts, which rebounds as lower interest rates on future debts. Living with integrity protects you from the temptation to fall for get rich quick schemes. Living with integrity builds the self-motivation and self-esteem to avoid laziness. Living with integrity helps you honestly assess the future as you plan. Living with integrity helps you remain steadfast in your work, and employers and investors are always looking to find and reward people who can be trusted. Living with integrity helps with the other six, and is a natural companion to success in the other six.

But living with integrity is also the wrapper around the other six, the context that helps keep the other six from becoming a new set of gods. Look again at what Solomon says about the value of integrity:

"A good name is to be more desired than great wealth, Favor is better than silver and gold." (Proverbs 22:1 NASB).

"Better is the poor who walks in his integrity, Than he who is crooked though he be rich." (Proverbs 28:6 NASB).

These are presented as statements of fact, not advice. Great wealth is not as good as a good name, and integrity+poor is better than crooked+rich. Recall that money is just an intermediate form, one way to transform your time and energy into your true desires. Your true desires ultimately have to be concerned with your character, with what kind of person you are. And money, to be any good to you at all, has to contribute to making you a better person. Getting money at the expense of becoming a worse person means that your money has failed.

It's a double-edged sword. If you compromise your integrity to get money, then you will find it harder to get, keep, and use money. You sacrificed your integrity to get money, and you end up with neither integrity nor money. However, if you focus on your integrity, then you will find it easier to get, keep, and use money. You make money subservient to your integrity, and you end up with both money and integrity.

I encourage you to think deeply about this principle, and let it grow to be bigger than all of your thoughts and feeling about money. God says that it is better to have integrity than riches. This is true, just like light follows God saying "let there be light." This is not just a lofty goal, or a statement of high ideals. It **is** better to have integrity, even if you don't always see how everything works out.

Integrity goes to **who you are**, and that is eternal. Riches, money, silver, gold go to **what you have**. There's a lot of stuff in the universe, and your connection with your stuff is not eternal. God is more concerned with what kind of person you are than how much stuff happens to be in your name today. You should be, too.

THINGS THAT ARE BETTER THAN MONEY

Solomon had more money we could ever dream of, and yet he tells us several things that are better than money. Understanding this, and living by this, is essential to putting money in its rightful place.

Wisdom is better than money. Solomon tells us that nothing we can desire compares with wisdom, and that love of wisdom precedes wealth:

"How blessed is the man who finds wisdom And the man who gains understanding. For her profit is better than the profit of silver And her gain better than fine gold. She is more precious than jewels; And nothing you desire compares with her. Long life is in her right hand; In her left hand are riches and honor. Her ways are pleasant ways And all her paths are peace. She is a tree of life to those who take hold of her, And happy are all who hold her fast." (Proverbs 3:13-18 NASB).

"To endow those who love me [Wisdom] with wealth, That I may fill their treasuries." (Proverbs 8:21 NASB).

By wisdom a house is built, And by understanding it is established; And by knowledge the rooms are filled With all precious and pleasant riches. (Proverbs 24:3-4 NASB).

Knowledge is better than money. Solomon tells us directly that knowledge is better than the choicest gold:

"Take my instruction and not silver, And knowledge rather than choicest gold. For wisdom is better than jewels; And all desirable things cannot compare with her." (Proverbs 8:10-11 NASB).

Righteousness precedes money:

"He who trusts in his riches will fall, But the righteous will flourish like the green leaf." (Proverbs 11:28 NASB).

It's important to keep in mind the order of these statements. Wisdom is better, and wisdom and righteousness are prerequisites for wealth and flourishing (which are much more than "having lots of money"). You can't trick God, and pretend to be after wisdom when your real goal is riches. You can use Solomon's principles to acquire more money, but, if you've not acquired wisdom and knowledge, and righteousness, and you've not lived with integrity, then you've actually gotten the bad end of the deal. You have used Solomon's principles to acquire the least valuable thing, money, and left the most valuable things on the table.

The truth that ties all of Solomon's money principles together is that you need to seek wisdom, knowledge, righteousness, and integrity. Part of doing that includes following the wisdom and knowledge of Solomon's money principles. Part involves focusing on integrity before riches. A right relationship with money follows those. Freedom from debt, resistance to dishonest schemes, and overcoming laziness, are all natural results of that knowledge and wisdom. The ability and confidence to work, and the promise of having enough, and the wisdom to plan ahead and spend wisely, are all natural results of that knowledge and wisdom. God promises you enough money for what He wants you to do, and the main thing He wants you to do is to become knowledgeable, righteous, and wise.

MONEY IS TEMPORARY. YOU ARE ETERNAL

Keep in mind that who you are is eternal, what you have is not. There is a lot of stuff in the universe, God made it all, He can make more stuff if He wants more stuff. Your choices, your character, are what God is after. Live like God tells you to, and you are more likely to be productive at accomplishing what God wants. If you need money to do that, then you will also be more likely to have more money.

If you want to be more successful in economic dealings, read Proverbs, over and over. Other self-help or business books will even make more sense, as you recognize that all their good ideas were in Proverbs a long time ago.

APPENDIX – USING SPREADSHEETS TO PLAN YOUR WAY OUT OF DEBT

There are many tools available to analyze debt. I found simple spreadsheets to be the most useful, since I could tinker with them all I wanted. If you're familiar with spreadsheets (like Excel from Microsoft, or Numbers from Apple), then use your best techniques to analyze your debts. In case you need help getting started, here are a few ideas from my experience. I'll try to go step by step, but I assume you have basic competency with your spreadsheet program.

I started my sheet by listing the numbers that matter to each debt. I wanted to be able to input our regular payment, plus experiment with various extra payments. I also needed to track interest rates and charges simply. Of course, I wanted to see what happened to the balance each month. With that starting point, my simple spreadsheet started with 6 columns. I arranged them like this:

month	regular payment	extra payment	balance	interest	interest rate

If you're building your own spreadsheet to match mine, just type those labels into 6 cells in one row.

The next row represented the starting position, so I filled in the starting balance and the starting interest rate. This was month zero, since it represented the day we took out the loan. There was no regular payment or extra payment yet, so those columns had zeros in them. For a $1,000 debt at 3% interest (picking numbers so the illustrations will fit), the first two rows look like this:

month	regular payment	extra payment	balance	interest	interes t rate
0	-	-	1,000.00	-	3.00%

The next row represented our first payment, and is where you have to build in the math so the spreadsheet can work for you. Here's what it looks like:

month	regular payment	extra payment	balance	interest	interes t rate
0	-	-	1,000.00	-	3.00%
1	150.00		852.50	2.50	3.00%

Let's go one column at a time, describing how each cell is calculated. I added row (1, 2, 3) and column (A through F) labels so we can refer to individual cells.

	A	B	C	D	E	F
		regular	extra			interes
1	month	payment	payment	balance	interest	t rate
2	0	-	-	1,000.00	-	3.00%
3	=A2+1	150.00	-	=D2+E3-B3-C3	=D2*F3/12	=F2

The "month" column is just the previous month plus one. For the regular payment, just type in the regular or minimum payment amount. We'll leave the extra payment zero for now. For the interest box, we need to tell the spreadsheet how to calculate the interest each month. Each month's interest is the

94

balance from the previous month, times the monthly interest rate (1/12 of the annual rate). All that's left now is the balance calculation. This is not complicated: the balance for this month is just the balance from last month, plus the interest charge, minus our payments.

Once we have this row built, we just copy it into as many rows below as we need until the debt is paid off. Since the interest and balance boxes calculate based on the previous month's numbers, they automatically keep track of the declining balance each month.

With our example numbers, the debt is paid off by month 7 (since the balance after the month 6 payment is less than the regular payment planned for month 7).

month	regular payment	extra payment	balance	interest	interest rate
0	-	-	1,000.00	-	3.00%
1	150.00		852.50	2.50	3.00%
2	150.00		704.63	2.13	3.00%
3	150.00		556.39	1.76	3.00%
4	150.00		407.78	1.39	3.00%
5	150.00		258.80	1.02	3.00%
6	150.00		109.45	0.65	3.00%
7	150.00		-40.28	0.27	3.00%

Now comes the fun part. Let's see what happens when we add an extra payment at month 2:

month	regular payment	extra payment	balance	interest	interest rate
0	-	-	1,000.00	-	3.00%
1	150.00		852.50	2.50	3.00%
2	150.00	100.00	604.63	2.13	3.00%
3	150.00		456.14	1.51	3.00%
4	150.00		307.28	1.14	3.00%
5	150.00		158.05	0.77	3.00%
6	150.00		8.45	0.40	3.00%

Paying an extra 100 in month 2 decreases our month 5 balance from 258.80 to 158.05, so we pay the debt off almost one month early.

You can use the spreadsheet to see what happens if you pay an extra 20 per month, or put a gift or bonus into a loan payment, or even if you can negotiate a lower interest rate at some point. Our example was paid in just a few months, so there's not a lot you can do except pay the principal. For loans that are scheduled to be paid off over longer times, such as car loans, house loans, or credit card debt that you're not paying in full, increasing the regular payment and adding extra payments can cause pretty dramatic changes in balance and payoff times.

Build your own spreadsheets, and build your own plan for freedom from debt slavery.

www.ingramcontent.com/pod-product-compliance
Lightning Source LLC
Chambersburg PA
CBHW070827180526
45168CB00002B/755